I'M NOT MAD AT GOD

I'M NOT MAD AT GOD

by David Wilkerson

BETHANY FELLOWSHIP, INC.
Minneapolis, Minnesota

First Printing—August 1967
Second Printing—August 1967
Third Printing—September 1967

Printed in the United States of America
by the Printing Division of
Bethany Fellowship, Inc.

DEDICATION

To

MY FRIENDS

CONTENTS

MUZZLED

"Thou shalt not muzzle the mouth of the ox that treadeth out the corn" (I Cor. 9:9).

The secret of success for every Christian worker is found hidden in this verse. I consider this one of the most important truths the Holy Spirit has opened to me in all my ministry. It revolutionized my life and ministry, and I will never be the same as a result.

To muzzle means to fasten or cover the mouth to prevent action—*to bind the mouth*. Paraphrased, this verse reads: "Thou shalt not bind the mouth of the worker who labors in the harvest."

Paul the apostle discovered this verse in Deuteronomy 25:4, and through a revelation of the Holy Spirit took this truth far beyond the concept of money and finance—bringing to the church world one of the most relevant messages for modern man ever delivered.

Paul begins with a question: "Doth God take care for oxen? Or saith he it altogether for our sakes?" God's humanitarian law provided that oxen who tread at the corn mill should not be muzzled, but should freely partake of the corn they were treading. The laborer is worthy of his hire—even oxen. Paul was certain this verse was more than a reminder of God's care for oxen: he states emphatically, "No doubt about it in my mind—this is written for us today . . . there is a principle involved."

Jesus said: "Take my yoke upon you and learn of me. . . . My yoke is easy and my burden is light." Oxen wear yokes. In typology, Jesus made His disciples to represent oxen ploughing the field of the world.

It is so very clear that the Holy Spirit seeks, through the word of wisdom, to lead Christian workers into a state of mind free from all bondage, full of faith and hope. "He that ploweth should plow in hope; and . . . he that thresheth in hope should be partaker of his hope."

How many Christian workers today labor for the Lord only out of a sense of duty? How many have lost hope of ever reaping a real harvest, to be truly successful? How many plow away in certain harvest fields, bound and fettered because in their honest heart-searching they must admit they have not been a partaker of all they preach? I meet them in my travels all over the world. Servants of the Most High God that once commanded devils and moved mountains, now stand fearful and alone midst the ruins of a dying vision. They once testified to the world that all things are possible to them that believe, but today they wander aimlessly looking for that lost glory. Nothing is more tragic in my mind than to see a Christian worker who once had God's hand on his life— to stumble around in fear and indecision because he allowed himself to become muzzled.

My mother used to tell me, "David, don't let anything bring you under bondage. Don't get bound." Now I understand how important it is to labor with a free spirit. I must work for God fully persuaded that unseen forces are behind me to bring to pass all the promises. I must never lose hope! I must taste every truth I preach! I must test every divine secret in the proving ground of my own heart! I must not be dishonest by preaching a gospel I have not proven. It is not enough for me to say Paul said thus and so. I must be able to thunder from my own vantage point of experience, "I know what Paul was saying. I have walked the same path of revelation."

It is only a shortsighted view of this truth that suggests Paul is referring to better pay for those who live off the gospel. It is that, but so much more. It is in spiritual things we find the muzzle so devastating.

The twenty-fifth chapter of Matthew contains the perfect example of the muzzled minister. I suggest every born-again believer is a minister—called to be a witness for Christ. The story is simply told. A man, traveling into a far country, called his servants and deposited with them his goods. To one he gave five talents ($2,500), to another two ($1,000), and to another one talent ($500). After a long time the master returned to reckon with those in whom he had invested. This story is vital to every Christian worker because the master of this story is Christ the Lord; we, the servants who must give a detailed account of our actions when we are on our own.

Two servants stand before Him to face their finest hour. It is a happy occasion. They are well adjusted, fruitful workers who are able to say, "Master . . . I have made progress . . . I have gained. . ." The five-talent man and the two-talent man both doubled their accounts. No sweat; no foggy ideas about guidance; no mental blocks of anxiety or fear; no fearful stories about how the devil hounded them or how people were against them; no haggard demeanor; no defeatist philosophy; no excuses about the spirit of the age; no reference to having been placed in the hardest field in the country! These were men of purpose who knew they had it! Their job was simple and without complications: the master wanted results—and got them!

But now we focus attention on that maladjusted servant who stands before the master empty handed. The one-talent servant—he is the type of the *Muzzled Man!* Examine with me the three tragic steps that lead to a bound and fruitless ministry. If Bible statistics hold true, about one-third of God's servants will stand before the judgment bound and gagged—with no fruit. Beware of these three steps.

STEP NUMBER ONE: A WRONG RELATIONSHIP WITH THE LORD

Listen to his confession: "Lord, I knew thee . . . that thou art a hard man" (vs. 24). They all knew the Lord, but here was a servant who labored under a wrong relationship. Two servants had already demonstrated that the Lord was not difficult or hard to serve. But in this servant's mind—*He was hard!* This concept of a cruel, hard-driving Father is the chief propaganda of Satan.

Satan is subtle. He knows he cannot trap God's servants with vulgar temptations involving the misuse of money or immorality and sensuous pleasures. The enemy of our soul seeks to paint in our minds a picture of a fire-breathing, vengeful dictator in the sky—ready to breathe wrath on every child who disobeys or falters. The devil baited certain theologians with this line and they swallowed it hook, line, and sinker. They couldn't live with their mean God so they just buried Him; and in saying God is dead, they admit: "We just couldn't understand Him. He was too hard to handle."

I came to New York City with a broken heart and my entire ministry to delinquents was based on the scripture: "He that goeth forth and weepeth, bearing precious seed, shall doubtless come again with rejoicing, bringing his sheaves with him." I well remember those first months of ministry. I slept in my car because I had no money to sleep elsewhere. I knew no one. I was a naive country preacher—but I felt a divine glow and urgency. I walked the streets in the wee hours praying for souls and for guidance. In those months of reaching gangs on a person-to-person basis, no temptation could touch me. The prostitutes and the promiscuous took one look at me and fled in fear. Every seeming failure and discouragement was only a stepping stone to greater victories. But Satan was not about to let this important ministry go unchallenged. In a few short weeks and before I knew how it happened—my relationship with the Lord became strained.

It all started with a tragedy. I was scheduled to conduct a weekend series of meetings with a fine young pastor in a small town. I arrived shortly after an ambulance—with sirens wailing—pulled away from the pastor's parsonage. A distressed woman stood at the door, sobbing and wringing her hands. I was told that the minister, his wife, and little child were all in the ambulance headed for the hospital. Less than an hour later I arrived at the hospital to find out what had happened.

After an introduction, the pastor took me into a private room and pointed to a small child lying unconscious in an oxygen tent. Faint tire marks were visible over her face. "Who's child?" I asked. "She's mine, Brother David," said the pastor. "I rushed out of the house because I was late for a funeral. I didn't know she was playing under the car—I ran over her." The sight of a weeping minister, his hysterical wife, and the unconscious child was shocking and unnerving. I have never prayed more diligently for anyone in all my life. But behind the prayer a blanket of fear had already fallen on my heart. I was questioning God . . . "Why?"

I was still asking that question when I viewed the lovely child in the funeral parlor. She looked like an angel. I glanced over at the father and mother and, taking one final look at the child, gritted my teeth and whispered, "God, don't ever strike my home with this kind of judgment. I'll do anything you ask me to do—just don't touch one of my children." It started that moment, standing before that child's casket. A terrible thought possessed my mind: "He must have committed some terrible sin to deserve such punishment." My concept of God suddenly began to change.

I rushed home to my wife and children, gathered them in my arms and under my breath said, "God, I'll give my life for the gangs in New York, but don't ever take one of my children." Gwen was expecting our third child. I had not been with her when Debbie and Bonnie were born, and she wanted me with her just once. I had scheduled a crusade for delinquents at St. Nicholas' Arena and this necessitated my going to the city, some 400 miles away, each week for two or three days. I was still pastoring the small church in Pennsylvania. She begged me not to go this time; she felt I was desperately needed at home. "I must go, honey—or the child could be born crippled if I don't obey God and fulfill my call." I did go. But this time I went bound in the spirit. I was no longer free. Oh, I still knew the Lord—but now as a Hard Man!

When I returned, Gwen was not there to

meet me at the door as usual. I found her in bed in a near state of shock and unaware that I was in the room. As I stood over her a scripture rang through the corridors of my mind so loud and clear I was taken aback: "A man who neglects his own household is worse than an infidel and has denied the faith." I fell to my knees and asked God to touch and heal her. She fell asleep.

I slipped quietly into my study, spread a blanket on the floor and began to pour out my heart to God. The heavens were brass. The yoke was not easy and the burden was too heavy. I wept through tears of sorrow, wonderment, and self-pity. I had not smiled in days. I was determined to "have it out with God on the spot." Suddenly a blackness I dare not even try to describe came over me. It was as though the angel of death was breathing on the back of my neck.

"Stand up," a still, small voice commanded. Then came a torrent of accusations: "You're going to New York only to seek fame. You want to be somebody. You're a fake. Your wife will lose her mind and baby. God will judge you for a heart full of pride." I fell to my knees, quaking and shaking. "No, God!" I screamed. "It's not true . . . I love you . . . I've given all . . . you can't possibly think so bad of me after all

17

I've gone through—kicked out of court . . . they call me skinny fanatic—what's it all about?"

Then a ray of light came through in the form of a scripture verse: "Try the spirits to see if they are of God." Another verse came to mind, "If any man sin, we have an advocate with the Father." I stood to my feet, looked up and prayed, "God, I don't believe these lies, but even if they are true, you are my advocate; Jesus, forgive me."

The voice began to curse, and I knew it was the accuser of the brethren—Satan. I began to laugh. The load began to lift; the darkness vanished. I ran into the children's room where Debbie and Bonnie were sleeping in bunk beds. From the top bunk I gathered Debbie in my arms and went into the living room. It was about two o'clock in the morning and she was fast asleep. But she was so starved for Daddy's affection she clung like a vine. In the middle of the room, I seemed to hear a voice say, *"Drop her—let her go!"* I held even tighter and said out loud, "Never. She's my girl. I'll never drop her—never let her go." As clear as any still, small voice, I heard, "Yes, and you are My son. I'll not drop you. I'll never let you go or harm you." I began to see it all. I laid Debbie back in bed and began running through the house praising

God. A torrent of scriptures came pouring into my heart:

"If God marked iniquities, who among us could stand?"

"He knoweth our frame—He remembereth that we are but dust."

"My yoke is easy—my burden is light."

"His mercy and lovingkindness endureth forever."

I woke up my wife and told her the good news. "Honey, I'm not mad at God any more, and He's not mad at me. My relationship is all right now."

I have felt and known His love. I am no better than before, but there is no power on earth or in hell that can separate me from this relationship of love and mercy. I have failed Him many times since, but in the midst of it all I have rested in the constant love relationship between us.

STEP NUMBER TWO: A FEAR COMPLEX

"So I was afraid" (vs. 25). A wrong relationship with the Lord always breeds fear. Fear is bondage. Fear hath torment, and this tormented servant was misled by a concept that is prevalent even today. This is the idea that God does not need me, a frail human being, to perform a job. He can do it by just speaking a miracle into being ("reaping where thou hast not sown and gathering where thou hast not strewed"). What this servant really meant was, "You can save the heathen without me. Why should I evangelize them? You have the power to save my loved ones by just an act of power. Why should I have to sweat and cry and pray?"

Everywhere I go today, I meet Christians who are bound by fears of all descriptions. Fear of pride, fear of the future, fear of failure, fear of losing one's mind, fear of past sins, fear of people, and many others. Wherever you got your fear—you didn't come by it through God. So why put up with it? The Word says, "God hath not given us the spirit of fear; but of power, and of love, and of a sound mind." A right relationship with the Lord is one of perfect love—and that drives out all fear. David said: *"I will fear no evil."*

A seminary student tells me his sermons seem to fall on the ground ten feet in front of the pulpit. A teen-age girl confesses, "I'm all bottled up inside. I pray and cry and read my Bible, but I'm bothered and frustrated. I'm tied up in knots inside." A mother tells me, "I've given all to the Lord, but I keep doubting. I can't seem to get through. I am tormented with fear."

Why? Why all the doubts and fears? Why are there so many today who know not how to live a life of real faith and victory? Because they are muzzled by fear! Until that fear, which is really unbelief, is driven out, man can never be a free soul. *Shake off your fears. They are all of the devil!* Don't put up with them!

STEP NUMBER THREE:
AN OBSESSION FOR SAFETY
AND SECURITY

". . . and went and hid thy talent in the earth" (vs. 25).

He had no adventurous spirit. He was afraid to risk for his master. Fear of competition led him to bury the talent. Rather than be out-bid by men of greater talents, he settled for security. He was playing it safe. He would console himself with the idea: If I can't do it, I won't be a hypocrite or a hero.

When men shall cry "peace and safety"— then shall the end come. When churches, ministers and Christian workers seek only to maintain the status quo—then shall the end be in sight! God uses men who are ready to risk everything —to step out in faith—to invest in vision—to launch out into the deep.

How many great things will never get done in God's work because laborers are trading their vision for security. Away with nest eggs; away with fears of "rainy days"; away with real estate agents who preach on the side; away with dabblers who won't move until they see the end from the beginning.

The love of security is addictive! It is a bottomless pit. It is a desire that can never be satisfied. Many are laid on the shelf and are useless to God's work because of this fly in the ointment.

I stepped out by faith to go to New York. I slept in a little office and began my ministry to teen-agers without a dollar in the bank account. God has never failed me. He has loaded me daily with His benefits. I have proven God. Step out by faith and you'll discover a new world of victory, glory, adventure and fruitfulness.

Cut off the muzzle! Get free! You need not be bound!

LESSON:

The secret of usefulness requires the following:

1. *A right relationship with the Lord.* A father-son relationship based on mutual love and communication.

2. *Freedom from all bondage*. Fear that binds can be cast out by the prayer of faith. Get to know what His love is because perfect love casts out all fear.
3. *A reckless abandonment to the faithfulness of God*. Look into the history of every great work God has raised up and you will find a man who was not afraid to risk everything to fulfill his call.

THE RESURRECTED LIFE

I quote from my diary, August 24, 1965: "After seven years of service to my Lord, I still do not fully comprehend the act of crucifixion and the resurrected life. I must know what it means to die, never to be heard from again."

Now let me tell you how that death came about—what God showed me the two hours previous to the moment of death.

I was walking to and fro in my study and crying aloud to God, "O Lord, crucify me, crucify me. Let me die. Let me live the crucified life." In my mind I was slowly walking toward Calvary, trying to recapture and relive those last moments with Christ at Calvary. I tried to imagine the suffering, the shame, the pain that Christ endured in my behalf. I tried to catch the sweeping glances of the faces that stood by mocking. I struggled to see them nail Him to His cross and then lift Him above the hill. I waited to hear the sound of thunder and see the bolts of lightning that signified that all heaven was viewing the scene. But there was no sound of thunder. Instead, loud and clear and ringing over the hills came the cry from the lips of the Savior, "It is finished."

Just that quick I found myself crying aloud,

"It is finished! His death is my death. I am dead with Christ. It is finished." Now it became clear and the light began to shine on my soul. Paul the apostle said, "We are made conformable to his death." By faith we must walk the same path, face our hour of trial, our accusers, and approach our cross and be crucified with Him. By faith we are to reckon it so.

Jesus did not live the crucified life. Crucifixion is an act, not a way of life. Thanks to Him the following truths that I had never fully understood now began to become real. Our crucifixion is completed—it is over—when we with Christ on our cross can cry out to the whole world, "It is finished!" We must recognize once and for all that Jesus completed the work—that it is not ours but His. The body of Christ was laid in the tomb; and on that resurrection morning, the Spirit of the Lord entered into that tomb with power and resurrection—Christ came forth alive in newness of life. The Bible says, "The same spirit that raised Christ from the dead shall also quicken your mortal bodies." Just think of it. The very same Spirit that entered that tomb, that quickened the body of our blessed Savior, is the very same Spirit who comes upon that child of God who reckons himself dead and can cry aloud, "It is finished," and quickens that mortal body and allows him to come forth in newness of life to live with resurrection power. We do not live the crucified life—we live the resurrected life. Crucifixion is the act that brings about the resurrected life. Paul the apostle did not die daily. I believe he died a thousand times a day. What Paul was really trying to say is that "Paul, the apostle, is my cross; and I remove him from the picture daily. I get Paul out of the way so that the Holy Spirit can work through me."

My struggle with crucifixion has ended. No more striving on my own merits. No more condemnation because I cannot live up to my expectations. It no longer shocks me when the old man comes around again to haunt me and to suggest that he is not really dead and that I have fooled my own heart. To me he is dead because he has been deposed. He is no longer the dictator. He no longer rules supreme on the throne of my heart. He is a man without a country. He is a man without influence. He is a man without power. He no longer captivates my personality. He has lost all reason to exist; and because he has lost my will, my personality and my motivation, he has lost everything that speaks of life. He can make all the noise he wants—but he is a dead man. He can make all the claims he chooses to—but he has no rights. He has no legal claim on me. He can accuse me; he can attempt to lie and deceive me; but as long as I am fully aware that he has no hold on me, he is dead. He cannot touch me. He cannot hurt me. He cannot claim me. He cannot use me. He cannot lead me. He cannot force me. He cannot deceive me.

Some people have the mistaken idea that when Jesus said, "Take up your cross and follow Me," He is asking us to keep walking toward Calvary. This would suggest that the crucifixion is held in the distance but never attainable. Will we never understand that the cross Jesus referred to was human nature with all of its frailties, with all of its burdens, with all of its temptations and with all of its restrictions? Will we never understand that Jesus is trying to tell us to take up our cross of weakness and inability and follow on in spite of it all? David Wilkerson is my biggest cross. I would never be able to do anything for God's glory if I continually looked inside my own heart. I would be convicted out of doing anything for God. I would see only my unworthiness. I would be bogged down by my past failures. I would be crushed by the fears of the unknown and the tomorrows. Yes, my friends, it's a cross to be human. It's a cross to recognize how weak you really are. But, this is the very vision of self to which we must die. Satan would be satisfied to have us become addicted to moments of introspection. He wants your unworthiness to be changed into unwillingness.

Calvary is very real to me. I have been there. I was there with Christ; but to me Calvary was a way out—it was a way of escape. It was the open door to a resurrected life of power and victory and joy and peace and fruitfulness. Jesus finally laid down His cross, but we find that so hard to do.

LESSON:

Crucifixion is an act, resurrection is a way of life. We must daily consider the cross and all it implies, but we must also comprehend the power and glory that is ours through the resurrection process. Think of it: *The very same Spirit that raised Christ from the dead also quickens our mortal bodies.*

COMMITTING THE SPIRIT

"Into thine hand I commit my spirit" (Ps. 31:5).

What do you do when in trouble? when your soul knows adversity? when shut up in the hands of the enemy? when your eye is consumed with grief and your soul and belly is in turmoil? when your strength faileth and hopes are consumed? when you feel reproach and fear? when you are forgotten as a dead man out of mind? when you consider yourself a broken vessel? when slander comes at you from all sides? when you feel "cut off" from before God's eyes? when the enemy lays snares and traps before you and every step is hounded by Satan?

David said, "I am in trouble so into thy hand I commit my spirit." There is nothing else you can do except "be of good courage, and he shall strengthen your heart, all ye that hope in the Lord."

LESSON:

When you cannot go another step, just commit your spirit into the hands of the Lord, be of good courage and wait for Him to send strength and help!

"Until the time that his word came: the word of the Lord tried him" (Ps. 105:19).

Let us see now how God prepares a person for a great work. Joseph was sent to Egypt to be a deliverer for the seed of Abraham. "He sent a man before them . . . he was laid in iron." A helpless slave bound by a chain he could not free himself from—on his way to the throne.

Yet far more trying than the bondage and humility of it all was the conflict in his soul resulting from his love for the Word. Until he received that which God had promised him, the Word of God tried him. This trial by the Word comes to all servants who seek to walk in truth.

The flagrant sins of old prophets are paraded before you. The severe thunderings against sin and weakness paralleled with admonitions that man is weak and cannot resist in his own power. One verse cries flee; another, stand still! One chapter produces hope and peace, another casts the reader into despair at the revelation of God's holiness and severity. A person lays hold of promises, then faces a trial by the Lord that makes him wonder if he has been just a victim of his own heart's devices.

LESSON:

The trial by the Word lasts only *until* God's set time to bless comes. There is a trial of faith, and the more you love God's Word, the more severe your trial will be!

THE WILL OF GOD

". . . assuredly gathering that the Lord had called us for to preach the gospel unto them" (Acts 16:10).

No other subject is more thoroughly discussed than finding the will of God. Christians spend a lifetime seeking a simple formula for discovering how to stay in the center of His will. In my work with hopeless addicts and criminals, it is absolutely imperative to know God's plan and will for every future program.

How to Find it?

I have boiled it all down to one simple paragraph. "The will of God grows on you." That which is of God will fasten itself on you and overpower and possess your entire being. That which is not of God will die—you will lose interest. But the plan of God will never die. The thing God wants you to do will become stronger each day in your thoughts, in your prayers, in your planning. It grows and grows!

LESSON:

There is no single formula for knowing God's will in specific matters. Complicating it causes only frustration. The will of God simply grows on you!

PROVING MAN

"God left him . . . to try him" (II Chron. 32:31).

We have become so preoccupied in proving God that we have not prepared our hearts for the great tests of life whereby God proves man. Could it be the great trial you are now facing, the burden you now carry, is actually God at work proving you? "God did prove Abraham . . . offer him there a burnt offering" (Gen. 22:1, 2). God proved an entire nation to find out what was really in its heart. "Thy God led thee these forty years in the wilderness, to humble thee, *and to prove thee*, to know what was in thine heart, whether thou wouldest keep his commandments, or no" (Deut. 8:2).

An amazing verse is II Chronicles 32:21, telling how God left a great king for a season to prove him. "God left him, to try him, that he might know all that was in his heart."

Often, while in the righteous pursuit of God's work, the steward of the Lord finds himself apparently forsaken—tried to the limits of endurance and left all alone to battle the forces of hell. Every man God has ever blessed has been proved in the same manner.

Do you find yourself in strange circumstances? Do you feel forsaken and alone? Do you fight a losing battle with an unpredictable enemy? These are signs pointing to the proving process.

Victory is always desired, but should you fail, remember: it is what you have left in your heart that God is interested in, your attitude after you have won or lost the lonely battle. Your devotion to Him in spite of failure is His desire.

LESSON:

Jesus has promised never to leave us nor forsake us. But the record of Scripture reveals there are seasons when the Father withdraws His presence to prove us. Even Christ experienced that lonely moment on the Cross. It is then our blessed Savior is most touched by the feeling of this infirmity—and He whispers, "I pray for thee, that thy faith fail not."

LEARN TO LIVE WITH YOUR CROSS

"Take up thy cross and follow me."

What is that cross? It is the flesh with its frailness and weakness. Take it up, move on in faith, and His strength will be made perfect in you. Add to this David's word in Psalm 38:4, "For mine iniquities are gone over my head; as an heavy burden they are too heavy for me."

Is your cross of self and sin too heavy? Has your cross of personal weakness become too involved—and far over your head? Then, my friend, *take up your cross and follow on*. He understands and is there beside you to lift the heavy burden!

LESSON:

David Wilkerson is my cross. I am my heaviest burden. We move on in spite of our horrible weakness, and rest in His righteousness and His cross!

RESTLESSNESS

1. David's heart panted after the Lord. He desired God above all things. His hope was in the Lord. He was truly sorry and repentant for his sin. Yet—his soul was restless! "I am troubled; I am bowed down greatly; I go mourning all the day long. . . . I have roared by reason of the disquietness of my heart" (Ps. 38:6, 8).

2. The solution is found in the next chapter (39:6, 7): "Surely every man walketh in a vain show: surely they are disquieted [restless] in vain: . . . Now, Lord, what wait I for? [or what do I really want?]. *My hope is in thee.*"

LESSON:

Most of our restlessness is a result of personal vanity. The solution is to fully understand what it means to be *in Him*—and rest there.

THE PARADOX OF
PREACHING RIGHTEOUSNESS

(Psalm 40)

The Paradox:

David preached righteousness while being compassed with innumerable evils. "I have preached righteousness in the great congregation: lo, I have not refrained my lips" (vs. 9). However, "innumerable evils have compassed me about; mine iniquities have compassed me about; mine iniquities have taken hold upon me, so that I am not able to look up; they are more than the hairs of mine head: therefore my heart faileth me" (vs. 12).

Do you see this great preacher of righteousness returning from delivering his sermon on holiness only to see the sinfulness of his own heart? He is in total despair!

LESSON:

We cannot preach holiness only by the measure of our own goodness. We must preach the whole counsel of God, even in the weakness and despair of our own failures! Preach holiness. Then, strive to practice it.

John 15:2 is a terrifying verse, at first glance, to all who desire to bear much fruit. "He purgeth it!" A purge sounds like a blood bath, a revolution, a fight or struggle. It sounds like an overpowering by a higher power over a lesser power. It is not! "Let not your heart be troubled, neither let it be afraid."

How are my own children purged? By my word and my command. It is obedience to my command that purges them and produces the fruit of blessing and approval. Hear the Master: "Now are ye clean through the word which I have spoken unto you."

LESSON:

Purging is a tender, delicate and loving operation by a careful vineyard keeper who anxiously guards every branch—lovingly. Fear it not! His cutting knife carves from tenderness. If there is any pain, He promises to heal.

WHAT KIND OF LOVE IS THIS?

"As the Father hath loved me, so have I loved you. CONTINUE ye in my love" (John 15:9).

The Father's love drove Jesus into a wilderness—after an inglorious birth. It led Him to cursing mobs and misunderstanding co-workers. It took Him to Jerusalem as a hero, then dropped Him as an imposter. It took Him before kings and rulers to be mocked and ridiculed as a pretender. This love left Him bleeding and dying on a cross. It drove Him to the despair of loneliness and brass heavens. This love left Him as a corpse in a sealed tomb. What kind of love is this? Has Jesus really offered us the same kind of love—over the same path? Yes, but here is love: "The same Spirit that raised Christ from the dead shall also quicken *your* mortal bodies."

LESSON:

The path of true love may be strewn with crosses—but its greatest reward is a *true resurrection*, making it possible for those who continue in it to live in a realm of eternal values.

HOLDING OUT TO THE END

"Pray for me—that I'll hold out to the end!"
What a tragedy—what a lack of faith! How
very unscriptural. "We are *more* than conquerors—through Christ." Not just conquerors who
squeeze through the battle as winners, left beat-
en. wounded and scarred. Not huffing, puffing,
winded warriors. No, never! We are *more* than
conquerors. We come through the battle with
more strength than when we went in. We come
out swinging—we come out shouting; vibrant,
full of faith and energy; not a bit weakened by
the enemy or the battle. The enemy shall not
exact an ounce of strength.

LESSON:

Every battle we enter with the forces of
the enemy is a time of energizing—a time to
receive *more than we had before.*

HOW TO CONQUER SECRET SIN

(II Corinthians 3:18)

Strive—study—work for years to find the true source of power over besetting sins, and you will ultimately have to come to this simple formula:

1. Sin must be overpowered by God's glory.
2. This overpowering power comes only through consistent prayer—beholding His face daily.
3. The closer you get to Jesus, the more His character will be the ruling force in your life—overruling and overpowering the enemy.

"We are changed unto the same image— from glory to glory—even as by the Spirit of the Lord."

LESSON:

We wish God would miraculously "pluck out" our besetting sins and set us free. Not so! We overcome step by step—becoming more like His image by daily *beholding*. Time and much prayer is needed for complete freedom.

UFO'S (Unidentified Flying Objects)

In the last days we are told to expect signs and wonders in the heavens. It started with "sputnik" and now includes amazing sightings by reputable airline pilots who claim they have seen space ships. It is not the place of God's children to join in speculation on these unseen and unexplainable matters. As time goes by, Jeremiah 10:2 will seem vital to all of us. "Thus saith the Lord, Learn not the way of the heathen, and be not dismayed at the signs of heaven. For the heathen are dismayed at them." Nothing can separate us from His love, not even "any other creature" (Rom. 8:39).

LESSON:

As a nation rejects God and turns to heathenism, it turns with fear and homage to signs in the heavens. Eventually its only supernatural phenomenon is in the wonders of UFO's.

KNOWING THE MASTER'S VOICE

"My sheep know my voice—they hear when I call. A stranger will they not follow, for they know not the sound of his voice" (John 10).

Is it possible to really know when the Lord is speaking? Can we be sure it is not the enemy? All the Word of God leads us to believe that our Lord desires to speak clearly to His children—daily, frequently, and on every matter!

LESSON:

Three tests to determine His voice are:

1. *He speaks with a familiar sound*—no tension, strangeness or harshness. His voice is soft, sure, and constant.
2. *He always speaks in loving guidance.* He never condemns His children. He speaks softly and tenderly; never does He take away our victory or peace. Even when He speaks negatively, it is with love and kindness.
3. *His voice causes great rejoicing!* "The bride hath the bridegroom, but the friend that standeth nearby rejoiceth *greatly* at the sound of his voice."

GOD IS NOT GIVING ANY MORE!

"In him dwelleth all the fulness of the God-head bodily" (Col. 2:9).

God has given to Christ all things. Christ dwells in us as possessor of all things. Under His feet—so under ours. All things are already ours, for they are His. How can God give again what He has already given? The kingdom of God—the storehouse, the right hand of the Father—is all within us. He has made us to sit in heavenly places. Don't ever beg God for those things already freely given in Him. Appropriate all you need. It works!

LESSON:

The secret of getting things from God is to understand what has already been given—then take it by faith. This is the faith that pleases God.

THE CRUCIFIED LIFE OR
THE RESURRECTED LIFE?

For years I struggled to comprehend the crucified life. After a year of search and desperate prayer, God showed me this:

1. Crucifixion is not a way of life—it is an act!
2. It is completed when I am conformed to His cross and cry by faith, "It is finished."
3. I am buried by faith and reckoning.
4. Then the same Spirit that raised Christ from the dead rushes into my mortal body and quickens me, enabling me to live the resurrected life.

LESSON:

It is impossible to live a crucified life. It is not scriptural. It tends only to bondage. We must pass on to the resurrected life of joy, victory and rest!

THE CHRISTIAN'S CREDIT CARD

"In the day of trouble, I will call upon thee; for thou wilt answer me" (Ps. 86:7).

No wonder David called on the Lord. Think of all the benefits from simply calling:

1. No good thing will He withhold.
2. He will speak peace to His people.
3. He shall give that which is good.
4. He shall set us in the way of His steps.
5. He shall rejoice in the soul of His servants.
6. He shall extend plenteous mercy.
7. He will give His strength to His servant.
8. He will grant a token for good to shame all His enemies.

LESSON:

The promises of God are always in the superlative. He does not just answer prayer. He answers exceedingly above all we ask. David asked for help out of trouble, and look at the list of blessings that came with the answer.

A LESSON ON GUIDANCE

Today I learned a great lesson about God's guidance. For three months I felt a strong impression to purchase a theater in which to hold services for the afflicted. It seemed I had heard from God and should go ahead. Suddenly—all went wrong. I lost interest, the funds were not available and I was left confused. Did I mistake God's guidance for me? Was I not sincere about obeying Him? In my desperation I asked God for a definite answer today. It came. The owner withdrew from negotiations, making my decision for me!

LESSON:

"The steps of a righteous man are *ordered* by the Lord." It has *all* been pre-planned. My confusion about guidance is related to my inability to hear! Things are working together for good. He has ordered it so. All I have to do is trust in His overruling providence.

AM I RESPONSIBLE?

"Lift up your eyes to the fields that are now whitened unto the harvest" (John 4:35).

I have just returned from the island of Haiti. I saw more hopeless poverty, blindness, and demon power than in all my ministry to drug addicts. I saw hundreds of abandoned, uncared-for children. Having lifted my eyes to this *new* field, should I not seek a harvest here too? Yes! I am responsible. Not for the orphans in Korea— I have not yet seen their need. But for these in Haiti, yes, I have seen that need!

LESSON:

A man who walks with God can never erase the sight of human need from his heart. He must act or forever shut his eyes. He cannot see and then be at ease. Vision carries with it a great obligation!

A MESSAGE TO THE POOR

"Give and it shall be given unto you; good measure, pressed down, and shaken together, and running over" (Luke 6:38).

Does that promise work? Does it apply only to the affluent? Can you imagine my surprise when the Spirit bade me preach this very message to the poverty-stricken saints in Haiti? Their average daily wage is fifty cents per day—yearly average less than seventy-five dollars. Some were shoeless—and all wore ridiculous-looking used clothing. At first it seemed a cruel joke, but soon I saw the light. Did not the widow's mite touch the heart of the Master? You can be assured that widow was rewarded. God's Word is true: give and it shall be given unto you. That is the secret of receiving—giving joyfully with no design on a return! I urged the Haitian Christians to give more of themselves and more from their want.

LESSON:

Poverty can be a curse resulting from a self-ishness—both personally and nationally. God promises to supply all our need. And that promise belongs to all poverty *victims* as well as the more fortunate.

VOODOO AND THE DOLLAR

"The love of money is the root of all evil"
(I Tim. 6:10).

But can it be the *root* of heathenish voodoo? Yes! Last week I interviewed Dictator Duvalier's personal voodoo priest (Honga). He confessed it was his love of money that led him into voodoo practice. His followers were all money-mad. Voodoo is the state religion in Haiti (unofficially). I saw more hands outstretched for dollars there than any other place I have visited. The nation has its big hand outstretched for the dollar. Satan has used this perverted love to enslave an entire nation. All the evils of poverty, superstition, immorality and voodoo is the result!

LESSON:

If the love of money can destroy a nation, can it not more effectually destroy an individual? *Flee this lust!* It is the root of *all* evil. It all begins here! It is the first step in all moral landslides.

"IS IT NOTHING TO YOU—
ALL YE THAT PASS BY?"

(Lamentations 1:12)

The prophet said, "Abroad the sword bereaveth, at home there is as death." There is a spiritual death in our nation today that is robbing us of our missionary zeal. The sword of famine, pestilence, demonism is bereaving missions—yet we are becoming powerless, for "at home, there is as death."

Awaken us, O God, from the slumber of ease and riches ere the sword devour us also.

Is it nothing to you, O man of God? You that pass by, what about the sword abroad—and the death at home?

LESSON:

Missionary vision is the simple matter of making God's business our own; His burden, ours!

PRINCIPAL PROMISES

"The promises of God are yea...and in him Amen, unto the glory of God by us" (II Cor. 1:20).

We are all prone to complain with David, "Hath God forgotten; hath his promises failed?" We exercise faith—we lay hold of the promise to obtain them—we press God in holy violence. But no apparent answer. What then? Look to the principal promises—the overruling promises:

1. "All things work together for good to them that love God, and are called."
2. "The steps of a righteous man are ordered by the Lord."
3. "Lo, I am with you always."

LESSON:

Satan can trick you only on the "small print." He cannot touch the servant who stands on God's overruling promises!

GOD IS NOT DEAD—JUST HIDING!

"Why standest thou afar off, O Lord? Why hidest thou thyself in times of trouble?" (Ps. 10:1).

Shame on you, David! You are a man after God's own heart! Just when I rebuke my generation for suggesting God is dead, I discover your tragic moment of unbelief. In your time of trouble you thought He was hiding! You listed three reasons for your trouble:

1. The proud wicked would not seek after God.
2. Your generation was full of deceit and fraud.
3. It was a generation who thought God was asleep.

This is the cause of my troubled soul! I confess too, David, that I have cried the same tragic notes. "God, are you hiding in our time of trouble?" Will He yet call me a man after His own heart?

LESSON:

God never hides himself in times of trouble—but His judgments are far above out of our sight (Ps. 10:5).

THE MESSAGE AT MIDNIGHT

"I will bless the Lord, who hath given me counsel; my reins also instruct me in the night seasons" (Ps. 16:7).

With David I can say my best instructions come after midnight. "Thou hast visited me *in the night;* thou hast tried me and shall find nothing; I am purposed that my mouth shall not transgress" (Ps. 17:3).

Here are three powerful results of midnight prayer and seeking:

1. A visit from God.
2. A heart searching.
3. A renewed purpose.

When David said "Early will I seek him," I believe he referred to his midnight meetings with the Lord. For those who cannot rise early at six or seven to pray, *stay up after midnight and pray earlier!*

LESSON:

If at midnight a cry is to be made, "Behold, he cometh," let us be found waiting. God's great events happen at midnight! *Midnight is God's hour!*

I AM WEAK

"Heal me, for my bones are vexed" (Ps. 6:2).

He slew a bear, a lion and a giant, but cries, "I am weak." He was vexed! He felt rebuked by God, chastened, pressed to tears. Powerless against a force that sought to cripple him— grieved by his own inability to rise above his tempter. Troubled by delayed deliverance— peeved at God for making no quick way of escape. Does it all sound familiar? Yes! It is my story and yours! Weak, sick, vexed. A revelation of a man's own weakness over self is deplorable and depressing. What to do? Repeat it over and over again, "I know He loves me. I am His."

LESSON:

Out of weakness one can rise to strength and power if he will not faint. The way out is a full revelation of God's love and care for His own!

OBEDIENCE IS BETTER THAN BLESSING

It is written, "Obedience is better than sac-
rifice." I say it is also better than blessing. This
is the deepest meaning in the story of Abram
offering Isaac on the altar. God said, "Go and
do this." He obeyed. Did Abram leave that
altar saying, "God changed His mind"? I don't
think so. God wanted only obedience. I have
just experienced that today. God told me to
negotiate and gave me every evidence that I
should claim a certain thing. I did. I did everything in my power to obtain it. But I didn't get
it! What now? Shall I question God? Shall I
doubt He spoke to me? Shall I believe Satan hin-
dered me? No! I sought the Lord diligently.
He said, "Do this," and I did it. I will rest
in the peace of obedience. It is better than blessing. God shows you only one side of the coin—
obedience.

LESSON:

The servant must obey without question!
That, too, is faith, when a Master commandeth
His servant to go, he goeth; to come, and he
cometh.

THE THOMAS PHILOSOPHY

"Except I shall see ... I will not believe"
(John 20:25).

Jesus said, "My sheep hear my voice." We desire to hear His voice for guidance and direction; we delight when He makes His voice known to us, but how often are we guilty of doubt about His voice? "Except we hear," we will not believe.

There are many times we must go on in total silence—total darkness—no light, no voices, just faith. I do not see, or hear, but I believe! I believe He is guiding, He is leading. All things are working together for good!

LESSON:

If you cannot understand, you can trust! Faith must never be subject to voices, leadings, dreams or visions. Faith stands alone on God's promise that *He Is!*

THE FAITH OF GIANTS

"Though he slay me, yet will I trust in him"
(Job 13:15).

Can a man purpose in his heart to trust God when it appears He is breaking promise? Can a man still speak the language of faith when all his leadings "blow up" in his face? The giants of faith did! Men of great faith faced the most fiery trials. God has peculiar ways of developing faith, and the deeper in God you go, the more peculiar will be your testing. Do not be led to think that afflictions are necessarily proof you are displeasing Him! Miracles are produced only amidst impossibilities. So you desire to be a child of faith—then ready yourself for a life of most peculiar testings.

LESSON:

Faith comes by using what you have. Don't wait for obstacles to be removed. Go forth anyhow! The most critical part of faith is "the *last half hour*."

FLEECING GOD

"Blessed are they that have not seen, and yet have believed" (John 20:29; see also Judges 6:37–40).

At an earlier stage of my ministry I was always "fleecing" God. Like Gideon, I wanted to feel the wet fleece. My faith was propped up by "evidences" and "happenings." This kind of faith is important to the weak, but it is imperfect. It is always looking for signs and tokens. God cannot disappoint the hope which He himself has begotten in us. If He causes us to hope in a promise, we are to believe it with nothing more than hope. No signs, no evidence, no happenings, no circumstantial proofs. Just commit it and come away with our minds no more sad.

LESSON:

A fleece is an immature maneuver of imperfect faith. Faith must depend on the Word— not on the wool.

DO YOU SPEAK OF HIM—OR TO HIM?

"Tarry ye here, and watch with me" (Matt. 26:38).

The true purpose of prayer is that we enjoy much personal communion with the Lord. The heart is reluctant to dwell in God's presence and satisfies its self instead with "devotions." This describes a hurried period late at night or early in the morning when a "quickie" prayer is offered and a hurried portion of scripture is partly absorbed. All the witnessing in the world cannot excuse a man from his duty and privilege of prayer in the secret closet. Locked in with God until the carnal soul is transformed! No man should pray without ploughing and no man should plough without praying.

LESSON:
Every gift from God will cost you a groan. True men of God feel too weak to face the enemy without daily, consistent praying.

OPEN DOORS AND ADVERSARIES

"For a great door and effectual is opened unto me, and there are many adversaries" (I Cor. 16:9).

"What lies just inside every open door?" Ask the children of Israel! "Giants—adversaries!" Men of God sweat through blood and tears just to stand on the threshold of an open, effectual door of service only to find the greatest battles are still to come. I can testify to the world that every open door God has placed before me has been accompanied by the greatest battles of my ministry. Every new book, every great crusade, has brought me new critics, more slander, libelous rumors—and ungracious treatment from ministers whom I believed to be my friends. They became my adversaries. Yet not one adversary has been able to close that open, effectual door. God has blessed in spite of it and the victory is all the sweeter.

LESSON:

Don't pray for open doors or to be effective until you are prepared to walk by faith through an army of adversaries. They represent the enemy's "barbed wire" defense.

ALL THIS AND JESUS TOO!

"For all things are yours. . ." (I Cor. 3:21).

A convert at Teen Challenge gave this wonderful summary of her experience since her deliverance from drugs. "It's so wonderful to be free and have Jesus too." What a glorious life in Christ! No vile habits, no heart of hate, no bondage or fear, no haunting memories of past sins—all this and Jesus too!

Answered prayer, peace of mind, a sense of fulfillment and purpose, kindhearted friends in the Spirit, joy beyond description, strength in trial—all this and Jesus too!

LESSON:

A Christian must learn to live a full life and enjoy the present. Enjoy all God's blessings He bestows and say, "All this and Jesus too!"

DISTURBED

"As an eagle stirreth her nest. . ." (Deut. 32:11).

The man God uses is often a restless man. He cannot be satisfied with the status quo. His nest is always being stirred. Just when he settles down to rest in a few months of enjoyable ministry, he loses heart or becomes strangely restless. He cannot tell you why. He may know the great joy of the Lord, but at the same time be absolutely disgusted with his present situation. Watch out—God is ready to break up the nest. You will soon be flung out into the space of faith and trust, ready to do God's bidding. All new ministries He has thrust me into have come immediately after a "nest stirring."

LESSON:
Restlessness and discontent are the motivation forces that drive all men of God to great heights of service.

"Before I was afflicted, I went astray; BUT NOW I have kept thy word" (Ps. 119:67).

I believe in healing. I believe in affliction. I believe in "healing afflictions." Any affliction that keeps me from going astray—that drives me deeper into His Word—is healing. God's most gracious healing force spiritually and physically can be afflictions. To suggest that pain and affliction are of the devil is to suggest that David was driven by the devil to seek God's Word. I have suffered great pain. I have called on God for deliverance and I believe Him for complete healing. Yet, while I go on believing, I continue to thank God for the present condition and let it serve to remind me how dependent on Him I really am. With David I can say, "It is good for me" (vs. 71).

LESSON:

Pain and affliction are not to be despised as coming from the devil. Such burdens have produced great men of faith and insight.

THE ELEVENTH COMMANDMENT

"Thou shalt remember all the way the Lord hath brought thee . . . lest thy heart be lifted up" (Deut. 8).

What is the greatest stimulant to my faith? What causes me to speak the Word and trust for the impossible? *Memories* . . . great memories. I look back at the testimony of experience. I remember the first miracle God performed for me. I think of thousands more—how He delivered in the face of overwhelming odds. A miracle is determined only by the odds against its happening: no odds—no miracles. When I survey the past, my faith soars. He who has not failed will not fail now. I have never been able to coast. In spite of all God has done, the heart is tempted to doubt. That is blasphemy when you consider the record. We must practice the Eleventh Commandment daily.

LESSON:

Faith is more than the evidence of things hoped for—it is the evidence of things received. It is the substance of promises enjoyed. Faith is based as much on the past as on the future.

THREE MAJOR PROMISES TO
A MINOR PROPHET

(Psalm 25)

When God first called me, I was praying daily in the woods. With the call to reach delinquents came these three promises. They are part of my inner man.

1. "What man is he that feareth the Lord? . . . him shall he teach in the path he shall choose." He has been my leader; in every path He has led me.

2. "His soul shall dwell at ease!" His burden has been easy and His yoke light. My soul never flutters.

3. "His seed shall inherit the earth." The gospel voice I give will be heard round the world. These promises are for all who want to be used. Only the Spirit can reveal it.

LESSON:

Every man God has ever used has anchored his soul and vision on great promises made personal and confirmed to his own soul by the Spirit.

FOLLOW-UP FAITH

"ALL THINGS, whatsoever ye shall ask..."
(Matt. 21:22).

I am discovering that my greatest need for faith comes right after a victory celebration. God comes through in answer to a desperate call. Prayer is answered. I rejoice and boast in God. Often the greatest test of my faith then begins. I believed God for the big need. Now, a dozen little needs crop up to support the very thing God gave me. Every staff member I have prayed into our organization by faith has needed a home, money to live on, a sense of direction. This requires great faith. In a way, supporting or follow-up faith is even more difficult. It involves so many small details. It is all too easy to exercise faith for big needs and fail in trusting God for the daily bread and guidance.

LESSON:

Our faith can move mountains, only to stumble over a pebble. There is a tyranny in small things. Beware of little foxes that spoil faith's vine.

CARES KEEP COMING ON

"Casting ALL your care upon him. . ."
(I Pet. 5:7).

Paul spoke of the "cares" of the churches that were thrust upon him. Every new-born church was another "care" on his shoulders. Growth, expansion, lengthening of stakes always involve new cares. The man God uses must have broad shoulders. He dare not shrink under the challenge of numerous cares and responsibilities. Every new step of faith God leads me to take has brought with it numerous new cares and problems. God knows just how many cares He can trust us with. It is not that He seeks to break us—in health or strength; it is only that *willing* laborers are few and the harvest is so great. Cares are taken from those who refuse them and given as gifts to those who are not afraid of them. Forget the case load you carry—can we not cast them *all* on Him?

LESSON:
Every new blessing is related to a family of cares. They cannot be divorced. You cannot learn to live with the blessing until you learn to live with the cares.

STICKS AND STONES MIGHT
BREAK MY BONES,
BUT NAMES CAN NEVER HURT ME

"And he cast stones at David" (II Sam. 16:5–13).

David appeared to be losing his ministry and the blessing of God. He had lost a son and a kingdom. A giant of God, a preacher of faith, appears to be groveling in the dust. He had just escaped treachery and mutiny at the hands of intimate friends and counselors—only to face the cursing, stone-throwing Shimei. "You devil—you are reaping the judgment of God. Things have gone wrong because you are a wicked man. You are a fraud."

David's faithful few were eager and willing to trace down and shut up this man and his gossiping tongue. "Why should this nobody slander so great a Somebody?" Let every man of God hear well the words of David to his associates. "So let him curse . . . God has allowed it . . . the Lord hath bidden him . . . the Lord may requite me good for his cursing this day."

David blessed God even for slanders. In his eyes, serious gossip and personal attacks against him would only serve to turn the tide in his favor.

LESSON:

One of the most important lessons soul winners must learn is to accept all slander and gossip as the inevitable price of leadership. Never try to chase off or revenge your accusers. Remember—all slander originates with those who seek revenge for having been "stripped" themselves.

OUR GOLDEN CALF?

Can you imagine an archaeologist of 2,000 years hence digging up the ruins of this barren materialistic age? What would they point to as representing the God we worshipped? The formless art? The meaningless steeple crosses? The gigantic rockets stored in deep silos underground? Would they be far wrong?

This is a generation with few real values. An age of phonies, cheap politics and insincere Christians. An age that seeks movement without grace and calls it music; money without purpose and calls it security; sex without sympathy and calls it love.

Let us not act bewildered by the apparent ignorance of those who danced around Aaron's golden calf. History will expose us for our ignorance and for falling at the feet of idols and golden calves far more ridiculous.

LESSON:

Spend all your time developing true values. Compromise and conformity form the base upon which golden calves are built.

LOYALTY

"...and say, The sword of the Lord and of Gideon" (Judges 7:18).

When the Scripture tells of ten men putting thousands to flight, I am sure it is a lesson on the power of loyalty and unity. Gideon's small army heard its leader cry boldly: "Look on me, and do likewise ... as I do, so shall ye do ... blow when I tell you and say, The Lord's sword *and of Gideon.*"

Both the Lord's name and Gideon's name rang over the battlefields that night. No church, no missions program, no organization can function successfully unless every worker is willing to come under both banners—the Lord's and the leader's! Let every disloyal soldier depart to his home. Cut him off quickly. Give no post to those who are not really in the camp. The power of communism is loyalty to a cause and to absolute leadership. The weakness of many Christian endeavors is half-hearted devotion to causes and disloyalty to leadership.

LESSON:

Gideon did not earn respect from his recruits —he demanded it. A man called to do a great work can not indulge in the luxury of "winning workers and influencing associates." He must gather to his side men bold and loyal. Loyalty is the foundation upon which all great works are built.

PRAYER—THE LONG AND SHORT OF IT!

"Be not rash with thy mouth, and let not thine heart be hasty to utter any thing before God; for God is in heaven, and thou upon earth: therefore let thy words be few" (Eccles. 5:2).

There is often a pretense in long prayers. A desire to build up "credit power" with God; an ambition to duplicate the prayer lives of men used of God; a subtle attempt to overwhelm the Lord with enough words to weary Him into action. I wonder—does God ever get bored? Does He long for more prayers and petitions framed with brevity and intelligence? Some of us go to the secret closet and just "run off at the mouth." We become rash, wordy, and parrot cliches, meaningless petitions and praise patterns. God deserves an intelligent, concise presentation of our needs, a clear-minded offering of sincere praise, and a dignity based on our respect for the King of all kings.

LESSON:

Be specific with God in prayer and He will be specific with you in regard to the answer. Nonchalance and levity have no place in His courts.

74

STAY WELL ADJUSTED

"For God hath not given us the spirit of fear; but of power, and of love, and of a sound mind" (II Tim. 1:7).

There is nothing more sad than a frustrated Christian. The ministry also has in its ranks men who cannot isolate their vision or their sphere of service. They cannot abide in their calling because they have never been fully persuaded what that call was.

Contrary to popular thinking, frustration in the Christian world is not necessarily the result of idleness and laziness. It is often caused by doing too much in the name of faith only through human love and zeal. It is absolutely necessary to understand the danger and disaster of "going out on a limb" on projects that may be good and honorable and needed, but without a clear mandate from God. Do only what God directs you to do, nothing else. The majority of our burdens that bring on frustration are our own—God never ordained we carry them.

LESSON:

Good things can lead to disaster if done only through human love and zeal. Refuse all burdens that are not ordained of God for you. Abide in your calling. Self-imposed burdens bring on nervous breakdowns.

"I WILL FEAR NO EVIL"

(Psalm 23)

List all your fears on a sheet of paper. Include the subtle fear of pride, of failure, of self-introspection, of death and pain. Then over them all write these words, "I will fear no evil." Satan seeks to keep our eyes on our past failures and present inner weaknesses. I have learned that the enemy flees in terror each time he tries to accuse me because I stand my ground in spite of all feelings of unworthiness, and with a nagging sense of unrighteousness I cry out, "I will fear no evil."

I don't know where you got your fear, but I know you didn't get it from the Lord. Why put up with it? Why be afraid? Why let evil or the thought of it frighten you?

LESSON:

Don't look backward, inward, or forward. Look only upward! The fear of the Lord is only the beginning of wisdom. Perfect love casteth out *all* fear.

IN CASE OF FLOOD

"When the enemy COMES IN LIKE A FLOOD..." (Isa. 59:19).

Can you picture those sunbathers on the beach of California when the tidal wave came and carried them away to their doom? There was no warning and it was beyond their power to resist. It was not just swift current—it was an ocean of water dumped over them in such force and magnitude they were just like toys tossed to the mercies of the elements.

The fiery darts of the enemy are only for those without real faith. They do not work against those who have learned the simple plan of God to quench them. For them Satan has reserved the flood! An instant—sudden—roaring—overpowering with every weapon in his arsenal. When you least expect an attack, *then he pours it on!* Suddenly without any warning—in a quiet moment—you find yourself in an overwhelming situation. You are grasping for your very spiritual life. Your soul is turbulent; your mind is confused. Almost against your will you find yourself being pushed into making a foolish move. You find yourself saying ridiculous things—thinking thoughts contrary to all you have ever stood for. *It is all a design of Satan.*

It is the flood, the purpose behind it all being to get a true child of God to do a foolish, rash thing that will destroy his effectiveness.

It is in the flood that men of high thoughts find themselves capable of low thinking. It is then great men do small things. A man suddenly comes to himself and says: "This is not the real me; I am not really like this!" Then comes the greatest trial—condemnation and self-depreciation. A man is driven to tell himself: *"How can God use me? Look how I have failed! I thought I was bigger than this. I thought I had passed this point. But I have acted like a child!"* This is all Satan wants. He wants you to look at your weaknesses you exposed in the middle of his floods.

Don't fall for it! It's a trick! It's a device of hell! You can't fight this kind of battle—it's too big for you. So stop! Rest! Assure your heart that you are being attacked—that the enemy is throwing all hell at you! But keep your mind cool! Don't panic! *The Spirit of the Lord will raise up a standard* (or put him to flight). *Resist him—he'll flee!*

LESSON:

When the devil comes in after you like a flood, just ride out the storm. Don't judge yourself on the basis of actions in the middle of this testing. He can never take you under the third time. Shout this in the face of the devil: "THE LORD SITTETH UPON THE FLOOD!" (Ps. 29:10).

"If thou hast run with the footman, and they have wearied thee, then how canst thou contend with horses? and if in the land of peace, wherein thou trustedst, they wearied thee, then how wilt thou do in the swelling of Jordan?" (Jer. 12:5).

I believe God allows lesser tests to prepare us for greater trials. The question is asked: "If you cannot fight successfully men on foot, in a safe environment, how can you expect to battle successfully with fierce warriors on horses, on the dangerous banks of the swelling Jordan?"

There is a great spiritual lesson here. If you are going to "cop-out" on every little test sent your way to prepare you in the skill of battle and resistance, how will you survive the trial that is coming on this age? How can you go through the fire when you flee even from the spark of conflict? Never pray to be delivered from your fiery test. He promised a way of escape through it, that you might bear it, thereby gaining strength and combat knowledge in this warfare against Satan.

The lesser tests in life will not make you immune to great trials, but they do serve the same purpose as the bear and the lion played in David's life—to prepare one to meet with giants!

LESSON:

Old soldiers of the Cross neither die nor fade away. They go from strength to strength, which means from test to test and victory to victory.

"I have finished the work thou hast given me to do" (John 17:4).

The hour had come! Jesus was about to depart from the earth. The last moments were spent in examining His ministry and effectiveness. Jesus listed three things He had accomplished before death. These are the very ministries I want to finish before I die.

1. *"I have glorified thee on the earth."* This is the only reason God calls anyone to work for Him—to get glory to His name. That must be our holy obsession—to design all we say and do to glorify the Father. I want my living and my dying to glorify His name.

2. *"I pray for them which thou hast given me."* Our most important ministry is to pray the same prayer for our loved ones that Jesus prayed for His: "Keep them through thy word.... Keep them from evil...." Unless you are ready to bear the burden of this ministry, you cannot know the blessing of the first mentioned.

3. *"For their sakes I sanctify myself...that they may be sanctified."* Any Christian who is fully persuaded that God has put His hand upon him must be totally set apart. He must

sanctify himself so that all who follow him and respect him may also be led into the deeper life. I must not allow any questionable thing in my life that may hinder the spiritual growth of a babe in Christ.

LESSON:

A man's death is in vain unless he finishes his work. It is not a sin to die with unfulfilled dreams—it is a sin not to dream. Our main work on earth is simply to glorify God.

THE "NOW" OF FAITH

"But I know, THAT EVEN NOW, whatsoever thou wilt ask of God, God will give it thee" (John 11:22).

Is it presumptuous to add *"even now, Lord,"* to your petition or request? Here is a woman who asks for a large thing—the raising of her brother from the dead, not on the resurrection morning, *but even now!* We have heard it said we dare not command God or place time limits upon Him. But God has always been a *now* reality. *Now* will I arise. Come *now,* let us reason together. *Now* the ax is laid to the root. Being *now* justified by His blood, we have *now* received the atonement. *Now* yield ye your members. Being *now* made free from sin. *Now* it is high time to awake. *Now* is our salvation nearer. The Spirit that *now* worketh in you. *Now* you are no more strangers. *Now* faith is the substance of things hoped for. *Now* faith has been the experience of every man who moves the heart of God. *Now* faith sets all heaven in motion.

LESSON:

If a man can come boldly into His presence and ask largely, why can he not also add, *"Even now Lord—you are able"*?

THE LOST VISION

In no area of our Christian life is Satan so anxious to muzzle us as in the matter of personal evangelism. He seeks to bind and render helpless every person who has experienced the joy of reaching lost souls on a person-to-person basis.

Have you lost your burden for soul winning? Have you been muzzled in this ministry? Test yourself against this list.

1. Are you afraid of reality and any stark expose of your hidden sins? any challenge that will jeopardize your present state of satisfaction?

2. Are you addicted to comfort, easy living, and permissible pleasure? Do you squeeze every ounce of enjoyment out of each and all legitimate pleasure?

3. Are you tranquilized by a false concept of rest and faith in God? Are you drugged by your own excuses for lack of power to witness and to pray? In seeking after a good God and a pitiful and merciful Savior, have you become overbearing in believing that the Lord will not deal severely with your lethargy and forsaking of your first love?

4. Are you set on fire by the sincere prayers from the lips of men who have done great things

for God, but then quench every spark of fire by getting involved in petty details and the little arrangements that life requires?

5. When you ought to be spending time praying, do you squander too much time figuring angles on how best to fight God's battles and win His victories? Have you often said that it is "not by might nor by power but by His Spirit"—then conveniently set aside this test and principle and embark on a course that depends on human abilities?

6. Was the call of God to a specific field and specific service once a dynamic, burning brand on your soul that also left its mark on everyone you knew? Is it now a spasmodic mechanical testimony that totters on a seesaw of indecision and fear?

7. Did the compassion of Christ at one time so possess your soul that praying was not a task or a burden, but a time of brokenhearted supplication for the lost and damned? Do you now struggle in your prayer life? Now must you force yourself into the closet? Do you find the initial burden you once had no longer glows?

8. Did you once have a holy boldness to preach to lost sinners any time—any place? Do you now have a professional shell that surrounds you and constantly pricks at your pride? Have you lately been satisfied with pulpit ora-

tory alone? Do you rationalize your lack of personal work by bringing into focus scriptures that infer only certain ones are called to do street work and front-line evangelism? Have you convinced yourself that you can do it and will do it when and if it is ever really put upon you? However, do you carry a secret desire that you will never have to do it as a ministry?

9. Do you rejoice greatly when others spend their hours talking to the lost on the street and as they go door to door, but somehow always manage to be occupied in another phase of ministry when it is time for you to join?

10. Do you preach witnessing to others, and even console your conscience by convincing your own heart that your ministry is to raise up and train others to do the job of witnessing?

11. Are you willing to attend all-night prayer meetings, stay up hours helping seekers to find the fullness of the Spirit, only to find it difficult to approach a sinner on the street? Do you testify about having power and courage and about wanting to do the perfect will of God, but yet have not fully proven that these principles work in and through your own life?

12. Are you bogged down with details, doubts, business, projects, activities and cannot find the time to set everything aside and "go out into

some highway or byway and compel someone to come in"?

13. Have you pitied and counseled poor, timid, fear-plagued souls but spent little time examining your own lack of boldness and faith?

14. Has your favorite expression always been, "Thank God for His many blessings in my life"? Did you share this testimony with those who really needed to hear it on the street?

15. Have others admired you on your desire for holiness? Are they persuaded that you are a sincere person of great faith; but in the quiet searching of your own heart, are you constantly aware of a struggle against self, pride, lust and fear?

16. Are you consummed with a desire to know the Lord better, to please Him more, to love Him with all your heart, and to do His perfect will, but do not seem to know how to enter in?

17. Do you know that His hand is on your life? Do you know He has used you much already? But do you seem to view the future apprehensively . . . unsure, undecided?

18. Do you want to prove God as the supplier of all your needs, but yet allow yourself to be constantly annoyed by persistent problems, worries, finances and perplexing situations?

19. Knowing all of this, do you also know that if any man sin, he has an Advocate with the Father? Do you confess your weaknesses to Him and cry for mercy? Do you know that if you are to be delivered from these great weaknesses you now face, He alone can do it? Do you rest your case and with a determined heart look to Him who is the Giver and Source of all life?

20. Does this sincere confession stir your soul and drive you to your knees with a broken heart? Can you cry out to God to deliver you from all your fears and to make you a mighty soul winner?